ARGENTINA

...in Pictures

Visual Geography Series®

ARGENTINA

...in Pictures

Prepared by
Geography Department

Lerner Publications Company
Minneapolis

Independent Picture Service

**Rarely dry, the eastern pampas provide abundant water for
animals, such as this horse who drinks from a pond.**

This book is an all-new edition in the Visual Geography Series. Previous editions were published by
Sterling Publishing Company, New York City. The
text, set in 10/12 Century Textbook, is fully revised
and updated, and new photographs, maps, charts, and
captions have been added.

LIBRARY OF CONGRESS CATALOGING-IN-PUBLICATION DATA

Argentina in pictures.

(Visual geography series)
Rev. ed. of: Argentina in pictures / prepared by E.W.
Egan.
Includes index.
Summary: An introduction to the geography, history,
government, people, and economy of the second largest
South American country.
1. Argentina. [1. Argentina] I. Egan, E. W. Argen-
tina in pictures. II. Lerner Publications Company.
Geography Dept. III. Series: Visual geography series
(Minneapolis, Minn.)
F2808.A6545   1988   982   87–3977
ISBN 0-8225-1807-4 (lib. bdg.)

International Standard Book Number: 0-8225-1807-4
Library of Congress Catalog Card Number: 87-3977

VISUAL GEOGRAPHY SERIES®

Publisher
Harry Jonas Lerner
Associate Publisher
Nancy M. Campbell
Executive Series Editor
Mary M. Rodgers
Assistant Series Editor
Gretchen Bratvold
Editorial Assistant
Nora W. Kniskern
Illustrations Editors
Nathan A. Haverstock
Karen A. Sirvaitis
Consultants/Contributors
Dr. Ruth F. Hale
Nathan A. Haverstock
Sandra K. Davis
Designer
Jim Simondet
Cartographer
Carol F. Barrett
Indexer
Kristine S. Schubert
Production Manager
Gary J. Hansen

Independent Picture Service

**Buenos Aires's business district resembles the commer-
cial centers of London and New York.**

Acknowledgments

Title page photo by Robert W. Nelson.

Elevation contours adapted from *The Times Atlas of
the World*, seventh comprehensive edition (New York:
Times Books, 1985).

3 4 5 6 7 8 9 10 97 96 95 94 93 92 91 90

At a cattle ranch on the pampas in Buenos Aires province, gauchos drive their livestock toward the paddock, where the animals will be weighed. Argentina is ranked fifth in the world for cattle production.

Contents

BOLIVIA

CHILE

PARAGUAY

BRAZIL

JUJUY

Pilcomayo R.

SALTA

FORMOSA

Paraguay R.

Tucumán — TUCUMAN

CHACO

Resistencia

CATAMARCA

Corrientes

Paraná R.

SANTIAGO
DEL ESTERO

CORRIENTES

LA RIOJA

Uruguay R.

MISIONES

SANTA
FE

SAN JUAN

Córdoba

PACIFIC

Santa Fe

Paraná

ENTRE
RIOS

SAN LUIS

Rosario

OCEAN

CORDOBA

URUGUAY

Mendoza

Chacabuco

MENDOZA

BUENOS AIRES

Rio de la Plata

La Plata

BUENOS AIRES

ATLANTIC OCEAN

LA PAMPA

Mar del Plata

NEUQUEN

Colorado R.

Bahía Blanca

Negro R.

Bahía Blanca

RIO NEGRO

Lake Nahuel Huapi

Gulf of San Matias

Salinas Grandes

Valdés Peninsula

Esquel

CHUBUT

Comodora
Rivadavia

Gulf of San Jorge

SANTA CRUZ

Bahía Grande

Port Stanley

FALKLAND ISLANDS
(ISLAS MALVINAS)

Strait of Magellan

TIERRA DEL FUEGO TERR.

Ushuaia

TIERRA DEL FUEGO IS.

Cape Horn

ARGENTINA

N

— Province Boundaries

0   300 Miles

0   300 Kilometers

80°   60°   40°

EQUATOR

0°   0°

PACIFIC

OCEAN

20°

ARGENTINA

SOUTH AMERICA

ATLANTIC

40°

OCEAN

0   1000 Miles

0   1000 Kilometers

METRIC CONVERSION CHART
To Find Approximate Equivalents

WHEN YOU KNOW:	MULTIPLY BY:	TO FIND:
AREA		
acres	0.41	hectares
square miles	2.59	square kilometers
CAPACITY		
gallons	3.79	liters
LENGTH		
feet	30.48	centimeters
yards	0.91	meters
miles	1.61	kilometers
MASS (weight)		
pounds	0.45	kilograms
tons	0.91	metric tons
VOLUME		
cubic yards	0.77	cubic meters
TEMPERATURE		
degrees Fahrenheit	0.56 (*after* subtracting 32)	degrees Celsius

ernal flame burns outside this
rnment building as a tribute to
de San Martín. An Argentine na-
¹ hero and liberator of southern
¹ America, San Martín was born
anish parents in Misiones prov-
He would later defeat the forces
ain in the struggle for inde-
ence.

Introduction

ated at the southern end of South
erica, Argentina is the continent's larg-
country after Brazil. Most of Argen-
¹'s people are of European descent, and
nation inherited many traditions from
Spanish colonizers.

ince gaining independence in 1816, Ar-
tina has experienced political instabili-
ty. Periods of civil strife and dictatorships
have alternated with stable leadership and
democratic reforms.

After World War II, Argentina was one
of the ten most prosperous nations in the
world. The country profited from its bump-
er crops of wheat, corn, and beef produced on the vast, fertile pampas (grassy

Tractors harvest wheat on this 7,500-acre estancia (estate) on the Argentine pampas near Chacabuco in Buenos Aires province. Argentina's fertile pampas have the potential both to meet domestic crop requirements and to export grain annually.

plains). The only threat to Argentina at that time was an ambitious army colonel, Juan Domingo Perón, who made himself president and changed the direction of the nation.

When Perón was elected president, Argentina stood at the beginning of an era in which the profits of farming would be used to promote industrialization. But, to achieve personal power, Perón disrupted the process by organizing strong labor unions before strong industries had been developed to support the unions.

Perón held the presidency for 10 years, from 1946 to 1955, before he was thrown out of office. During that period, Argentine workers enjoyed high wages and benefits beyond their dreams. Perón was assisted by his charismatic wife, Eva—or "Evita," as she was affectionately called by the Argentine workers who idolized her. When Evita died of cancer in 1952 at the age of 33, Argentine workers mourned her death as if she were a saint, because they were so grateful for their sudden material progress.

The governments that followed Perón found themselves with an impossible act to follow. They were unable to satisfy the expectations of workers or to deal with the disruptions in the Argentine economy caused by Perón's coddling of Argentine laborers—which had been at the expense of industrialization.

After almost 20 years of exile in Spain, Perón staged a comeback in 1973, when he was nearly 80 years old. Again he was elected president by Argentines who had not forgotten the prosperous years of his earlier administration. His third wife, Isabel, was elected vice president. In poor health, President Perón died the following year, and his wife became president in his stead—the Western Hemisphere's first female chief of state—until she was removed from office forcibly in 1976.

A series of military governments followed. Since the restoration of democracy in 1983, Argentines have looked to the future with more confidence. Their elected government is demanding sacrifice as a means of reviving an economy that they hope will become one of the most dynamic in the world.

Independent Picture Service

Centered in Buenos Aires's Plaza San Martín stands one of many monuments to José de San Martín. In the background lies the Río de la Plata, the estuary that forms the marine inlet between Uruguay and Argentina.

The Andes stretch across South America from the southern islands of Tierra del Fuego up to Panama in southern Central America. This mountain chain is the source of all of Argentina's large rivers, except the Paraná.

1) The Land

The Argentine Republic is the second largest country of South America, after Brazil. The nation stretches from the tropical wilderness of the Gran Chaco in the north to within 100 miles of Cape Horn, the chilly southern tip of the continent, near Antarctic waters. With 1,072,156 square miles, Argentina is nearly four times as large as the state of Texas.

Topography

Although people often think of Argentina only in terms of its pampas—the fertile grasslands that support some of the finest livestock in the world—the landscape of the country is dramatically varied and often beautiful. Running down Argentina's entire western boundary is a breathtaking chain of the Andes—a mountain range second in height only to the Himalayas of southern Asia—with snow-covered peaks and valleys choked with glacial ice. Near the border with Chile, Aconcagua, an extinct volcano, rises to a height of 22,834 feet. It is the highest mountain in the Western Hemisphere.

The broad lowlands of the Gran Chaco occupy most of northern Argentina before they thin out to the south, where they merge into the grasslands, or pampas, of the central region. Although the pampas cover only about one-fifth of the country, over half of the population resides in this region. Near the southern coast of Buenos Aires province, the level pampas are broken up by low mountain ridges rising to 3,000 feet above sea level and running west to east.

Farther south lies the great plateau of Patagonia, which covers more than one-fourth of the country. Finally, across the Strait of Magellan—the waterway at the southern tip of South America—the eastern half of the large island of Tierra del Fuego belongs to Argentina. Chile owns the western half, along with numerous lesser islands.

At 131 feet below sea level, Salinas Grandes (Great Salt Mines), on the Valdés Peninsula, is the lowest place on the South American continent. Lying on the northern coast of Patagonia, this peninsula is almost an island; it consists of a round

BOLIVIA

CHILE

PARAGUAY

BRAZIL

Pilcomayo R.

Paraguay R.

GRAN

CHACO

Paraná R.

Uruguay R.

MESOPOTAMIA

PACIFIC

Mt. Aconcagua

URUGUAY

ATLANTIC OCEAN

OCEAN

MOUNTAINS

ANDES

DRY   WET

Río de la Plata

THE PAMPAS

PAMPAS   PAMPAS

Colorado R.

Negro R.

Bahía Blanca

Lake Nahuel Huapi

Gulf of San Matías

Valdés Peninsula

PATAGONIA

Gulf of San Jorge

SAN JORGE BASIN

ARGENTINA   N ↑

Feet   Meters

19685 — 6000

16404 — 5000

13124 — 4000   Mountains

9843 — 3000

6562 — 2000

3281 — 1000   Uplands

1640 — 500   Lowlands

0   300 Miles

0   300 Kilometers

Bahía Grande

FALKLAND ISLANDS
(ISLAS MALVINAS)

Strait of Magellan

TIERRA DEL FUEGO IS.

Cape Horn

chunk of land connected to the mainland by a very thin land bridge.

Boundaries

Besides Chile, which shares Argentina's long western frontier in the Andes, the countries that border Argentina are Bolivia and Paraguay to the north, and Brazil and Uruguay to the northeast. The Bolivian border, like the Chilean boundary, lies in the Andes, and rivers divide Argentina from Paraguay, Brazil, and Uruguay.

From north to south the longest distance in Argentina is about 2,300 miles. The Atlantic Ocean delineates over 1,600 miles of coastline. Several large bays are located on the seacoast, the most important of which is formed by the Río de la Plata, which flows between Argentina and Uruguay. The Spanish name Río de la Plata translates as "River of Silver," but the river is actually an estuary—an arm of the sea at the lower end of a river. One of the great river systems of South America —the Paraná—empties into this estuary. South from the Río de la Plata, Argentina's coast is indented by a succession of wide-mouthed bays, including Bahía Blanca, Gulf of San Matías, Gulf of San Jorge, and Bahía Grande.

Driftwood lines the shores of a river in Patagonia, a region in southern Argentina. Early settlers regarded Patagonia as a desolate place inhabited by hostile Indians. Now, one of South America's most popular resort areas sits in western Patagonia.

Rivers and Lakes

The Paraná River system, which drains northern and much of central Argentina, has three main divisions—the Paraná, the Paraguay, and the Uruguay rivers, all of which rise in Brazil. The land between the Paraná and Uruguay rivers in the provinces of Entre Ríos and Corrientes is so fer-

A yacht is docked on the shores of Lake Nahuel Huapí, a popular resort area in the province of Neuquén. The lake, which is surrounded by mountains, boasts some of Argentina's most beautiful scenery.

Workers dredge, or deepen, the Paraná River by removing silt to keep the waterway open for navigation. The excavated material is sometimes used to build up low-lying ground.

tile that it has become known as the Argentine Mesopotamia. Entre Ríos, like Mesopotamia—the Fertile Crescent between the Tigris and Euphrates rivers in the Middle East—means "between rivers." In the Gran Chaco region northwest of Entre Ríos, vast swamps and lowlands surround the Paraguay River and its tributary, the Pilcomayo. The two rivers together form the boundary between Paraguay and Argentina.

To the south of this great system, the most important rivers are the Negro and the Colorado, which drain the eastern slopes of the Andes and flow eastward across northern Patagonia to the Atlantic Ocean. Both of these rivers actually rise within a relatively short distance of the Pacific Ocean. But because of the great Andean wall, they must flow to outlets in the Atlantic across hundreds of miles of arid regions to the east.

Another peculiar aspect of the drainage pattern of southern Argentina is a series of lakes that, under normal conditions, empty into the Pacific through the steep valleys of Chile. After heavy rains, however, these lakes send their excess water to the Atlantic. This phenomenon happens because the lakes are located almost on top of the continental divide (a line formed by the highest points on the continent that separates the waters flowing east from those that flow west). In the southern Andes lies the most beautiful of Argentine lakes—Nahuel Huapí—which is about 200 square miles in area and 2,500 feet above sea level.

Boaters cruise along this Buenos Aires marina. The capital city borders the east coast and enjoys a temperate climate, making water sports possible throughout the year.

Courtesy of Minneapolis Public Library and Information Center

Independent Picture Service

A bridge spans a dry bed where a stream once flowed in the northwestern province of Salta, a region that experiences an arid winter season.

This hydroelectric dam borders the Andes at Esquel in Chubut province. Hydroelectric sources produce approximately two-fifths of Argentina's power.

Climate

Most of Argentina is in the temperate, or mild, zone, but temperatures vary considerably. The Andean regions are cool in the north and quite cold in the south. The northern lowlands are tropical, while the central lowlands and the pampas have a moderate climate, similar to that of southern Europe. In the arid region of Patagonia, winds blow and temperatures drop as one moves south. Although there is no real summer in Patagonia, winters are rarely severe. One of the least inviting parts of the country, Tierra del Fuego, is cold and foggy, but ocean currents make the climate less severe, especially near the coast.

In general, rainfall lessens moving inland toward the Andes. Clouds from the Atlantic discharge most of their water by the time they reach the towering mountains, and clouds from the Pacific pour their rain upon the western, or Chilean,

15

Argentines strip yerba mate leaves from a holly tree and gather them into bales. Consumers eventually will steep the leaves to make tea.

A city workman pours yerba mate, or Paraguay tea, a South American drink that Argentines have adopted. Holding the traditional gourd, he will sip the tea through a silver straw called a bombilla.

side of the mountains, with little left over for the Argentine plains. Consequently, most of western Argentina tends to be dry. Its rivers often disappear into salt flats, and its parched foothills have little value for farming or livestock raising. As a result, the central plain is divided into wet and dry, or eastern and western, pampas.

Since Argentina lies wholly in the Southern Hemisphere, January is the warmest month and July is the coldest. The winter months—June, July, and August—are also the driest. The climate of the heavily populated east central region is mild and refreshing throughout the year, averaging in the low seventies in the summer and the high forties in the winter.

Flora

In the lush forests of the northeast that border on Paraguay and Brazil, many species of tropical and subtropical plants grow. Besides hardwood trees, a species of araucaria—a tall evergreen with large, edible nuts—is found.

The northern lowlands also support varied plant life. In the east a typical plant—and an important one in everyday Argentine life—is the yerba maté, a kind of holly whose leaves are used to make tea. Westward in the Gran Chaco, open savannas (treeless plains) alternate with scrub woodland. An important tree of this region is the red quebracho, whose bark and wood furnish tannin, an essential substance in treating leather. The quebracho's hard wood is also used for making posts and railroad ties.

Except where planted by farmers and ranchers to provide beauty and shade, trees are rare on the pampas. This vast area was originally one great expanse of tall grass that thinned to the west, where it gave way to the thorny brush of the arid belt.

In Patagonia short desert shrubs that are able to withstand both drought and wind dot the plateau. Occasionally, stunted trees are also found, blown into strange, twisted shapes by the wind. Walls of poplars have been planted as windbreaks in this region. Herds of sheep feed off of grasses that grow in the river valleys, where most of Patagonia's scanty population is clustered.

Except for some areas in the far north where cactus scrub prevails, dense forests cover the entire length of the Argentine Andes. Elsewhere in the northern Andes, where rain is plentiful, large stands of trees, notably the yewlike podocarpus, thrive. Southward the high-altitude forest consists of both conifers (evergreens) and deciduous (leaf-shedding) trees. The Chilean arborvitae and cypress trees are the most common evergreens, and the false beech is a typical deciduous tree of the region.

Fauna

Argentina shares with the rest of southern South America a relative scarcity of large land animals. The two largest—the vegetarian tapir and the meat-eating jaguar —roam in northern Argentina, where the greatest variety of the country's wildlife lives. Other warm-climate animals known in the wilder reaches of the Paraná and Paraguay river basins are the howler monkey, the giant anteater, and the pig-sized capybara—the world's largest rodent. In nearly all parts of the country the puma,

A man prepares pine seedlings for planting as part of a national program to help rebuild some of Argentina's forest resources.

Native to the Andes, the alpaca *(near left)* and vicuña *(far left)* belong to the camel family. Both are prized for their hides and wool. Vicuñas remain undomesticated, but alpacas are often herded in flocks.

or mountain lion, can be found. This yellow-furred predator is only about half the size of the jaguar, which is the largest member of the cat family in the Americas.

In the Andes and in the dry plateaus and plains adjoining them, the most distinctive animals are the ostrichlike rhea and the guanaco, a small, humpless, New World relative of the camel. These two species often run together, along with deer, in mixed herds on the plains. Llamas, alpacas, and vicuñas—all descendants of the guanaco—roam the northern Andean plateaus.

Patagonia and the pampas are home to many rodent species. The Patagonian cavy —with its long legs and a rather harelike appearance—is related to the guinea pig. Like the North American prairie dog, the viscacha of the Argentine pampas burrows enormous underground networks. Many horses have broken their legs plunging into one of these burrows, causing their riders to curse the viscacha. Wild dogs and red foxes also roam this region, and sea lions and elephant seals are native to the coast.

Argentina's various birds include the crested screamer (a running bird of the plains) and the tinamou—a prized game bird that resembles a grouse but that is actually a member of the ostrich family. Tropical species reside in the northern forests, while the albatross (a large, web-footed seabird) and the penguin are found along the southern coast. Occasionally the condor—a very large vulture—is seen flying high over the Andes.

Natural Resources

The greatest resources of Argentina are its expansive grazing lands and its fertile topsoil. The vast pampas are home to one of the largest and finest cattle industries in the world, and one of the best grain-producing regions of the globe lies between the Paraná and Uruguay rivers.

Although Argentina and its great La Plata estuary both bear names that mean silver, the country is not a major source of this metal. Metallic mineral deposits in general tend to be small and have never been mined extensively. Of the metals the country does mine, lead ores account for more than half, followed by zinc, tin, copper, iron, and manganese.

Oil has been drilled profitably from layers in the earth since the beginning of the twentieth century, mainly in the vicinity of Comodoro Rivadavia in Patagonia, where the Gulf of San Jorge supplies almost half of the oil produced in the nation. From Tierra del Fuego, plentiful quantities of natural gas flow by pipeline to Buenos Aires. Gas is also produced in the Mendoza area. By the mid-1980s Argentina had become more than 90 percent self-sufficient in petroleum. Both uranium—used in nuclear power—and coal are also exploited as sources of fuel.

Buenos Aires

The capital and largest city of the Argentine Republic is Buenos Aires. This world-class commercial hub is situated on the Río de la Plata, where the pampas meet the sea. A city of broad boulevards and spacious squares, its architecture recalls

Cattle, the backbone of Argentina's economy, huddle in an agricultural experiment station where scientists conduct research in breeding.

Independent Picture Service

19

Buenos Aires, the capital of Argentina, is characterized by many boulevards—such as Ninth of July Avenue *(above)*, one of the world's widest streets—that are reminiscent of Paris, France. Approximately 10 million people reside in greater Buenos Aires *(below)*, making it the fourth largest metropolitan area in the world.

those parts of Paris that were built in the late nineteenth and early twentieth centuries. During those years Buenos Aires grew from a minor capital to a metropolis and European immigrants looked to France for cultural inspiration.

Founded in the sixteenth century, Buenos Aires began as a colonial village of adobe houses surrounding a large, central square. The square, called the Plaza de Mayo, still exists, though little else of the colonial era has been maintained in the modern city. Among the colonial remnants are the Cabildo, which served as the town hall, and the Casa Rosada, or Pink House, where the Argentine president conducts official business.

The focal point of Argentine industry, education, culture, and science, Buenos Aires is a city of enormous vitality. The capital serves as the main seaport and financial center of Argentina and exports most of the country's beef, hides, mutton, wool, wheat, maize (corn), and flax (a plant that yields a strong, woody fiber used in rope and fabric).

Opposite Buenos Aires, the Río de la Plata narrows to about 25 miles wide. The estuary is formed by the Paraná and Uruguay rivers and lies between Argentina and Uruguay. Approximately 171 miles long, this large body of water stretches as wide as 138 miles at its mouth on the Atlantic Ocean.

Courtesy of Inter-American Development Bank

Throughout Buenos Aires, the government is replacing shacks with low-rent, high-rise apartment buildings. Argentines refer to the slums as misery towns. Shanties such as these house mostly migrants from the country's interior.

Approximately three million people live within the city limits of Buenos Aires, and the greater metropolitan area has a population of over 10 million. Although former president Juan Domingo Perón stimulated the construction of low-rental housing after World War II, adequate housing for low-income groups remains a serious problem in Buenos Aires and other large cities. Nevertheless, residents of the area enjoy the city's fine parks, public gardens, and tree-lined streets, as well as the advantages of a delightful climate, to which the city owes its name—Buenos Aires means "good air" in Spanish.

Secondary Cities

Centrally situated between the pampas and the foothills of the Andes, Córdoba is the commercial capital of the northwest. It is a bustling market for grain, cattle, and fruit and an increasingly industrial city. Córdoba's population of 984,000 people makes it the second largest city in Argentina. Rosario—midway between Buenos Aires and Córdoba—is the nation's third largest city, with a population of 957,300. Situated on the Paraná River, Rosario ships grain, hides, meat, and flaxseed from its busy wharves, and its factories mill flour, refine sugar, and process meat.

Freighters from all over the world dock at a port in Buenos Aires on the vast estuary of the Río de la Plata.

Mar del Plata, a coastal resort city in the province of Buenos Aires, attracts approximately two million visitors each summer. After tourism, fishing and food processing are Mar del Plata's most important industries. Fishermen land a host of marine life—including squid, cuttlefish, and octopus—at this major port.

La Plata (population 564,750), just south of Buenos Aires, is a relatively new city. Laid out in the 1880s, La Plata quickly became the capital of Buenos Aires province and thus removed some of the administrative burdens from the city of Buenos Aires. During his dictatorship, Juan Domingo Perón renamed the city Eva Perón, in homage to his second wife, but after the downfall of Perón in 1955, the old name was restored.

Mar del Plata, on the Atlantic coast south of the Río de la Plata, is a well-known resort, seaport, and food-processing city with 414,700 inhabitants. Mendoza, lying deep in the arid western uplands, is known for its vineyards, where much of Argentina's substantial output of wine is produced. With a population of 605,600, the city is surrounded by large areas of irrigated farmland. Several hundred miles to the north of Mendoza, the city of Tucumán (population 498,600) also lies in an area of irrigated farms, whose chief crop is sugarcane.

Other important cities include Resistencia, Corrientes, and Bahía Blanca. The finest natural port in Argentina, Bahía Blanca was long held back from full development by its remoteness from the main concentration of people and industry to the north. Recently, however, Bahía Blanca (population 223,800) has become a principal outlet for the oil of Patagonia. Ushuaia, while not a city, is the capital of the federal territory of Tierra del Fuego. The recent establishment of an electronics industry brought the town's population up to about 25,000 people. Ushuaia claims to be the southernmost town in the world, since the few communities that lie farther south are mere hamlets.

A bridge over the Paraná River connects Resistencia and Corrientes, two important commercial cities in northern Argentina.

Photo by Robert M. Levine

An Indian prays at a cemetery in Patagonia. Although the Indian population in Argentina was never very large compared to other South American countries, the nation's pure-blooded native population now numbers only about 50,000. Many died from foreign diseases carried by colonial settlers.

2) History and Government

The first recorded visit by Europeans to Argentina took place in 1516, when Juan Díaz de Solís entered the Río de la Plata and claimed the territory for Spain. In 1520 Portuguese explorer Ferdinand Magellan, who was sailing for Spain, stopped at the Río de la Plata on his historic voyage around the world.

Six years later Sebastian Cabot, an Italian in the service of Spain, sailed into the estuary and up the Paraná River. He established the first temporary European settlement on Argentine soil, not far from the site of the present city of Rosario. Cabot found the native Indians wearing silver ornaments and believed extensive silver deposits would be found in the area. Hence, he named the estuary Río de la Plata (River of Silver) in place of the earlier name, Río de Solís.

Spanish colonization began in earnest after Francisco Pizarro conquered the Inca Empire of Peru in 1532. Of the many expeditions to South America that followed that historic conquest, one resulted in a temporary settlement on the site of Buenos Aires in 1536. Constant attack by the Indians, by famine, and by disease, however, led to the abandonment of the colony in 1541. Strangely, most of the Spaniards who settled within present-day Argentina came over the mountains from Peru and Chile, rather than coming by ship directly from Spain.

Colonial Period

Following the abandonment of Buenos Aires, Argentine lands were initially governed from the permanent colony at Asunción, in what is now Paraguay. Tucumán was founded in 1565 and Córdoba in 1573 by colonists from Peru. It was not until 1580 that Juan de Garay from Asunción

Independent Picture Service

Hides, one of Argentina's chief exports, are lifted aboard a freighter at a dock in Buenos Aires, a free port city since 1776. After Spain opened the port to transatlantic trade, the city began to grow rapidly.

established a lasting settlement at Buenos Aires. By that time Spain had organized all of its South American colonies into a viceroyalty governed from Peru, and Argentina fell under the control of a subdivision of that vast realm with headquarters in what is now Bolivia. Argentine-born descendants of early colonists, called Creoles, were given little voice in this government run by Spaniards born in Spain.

The Spaniards imposed severe restrictions on trade and on the movement of goods in South America. Shipping was banned from the Río de la Plata, which meant that products such as hides and tallow from Buenos Aires's thriving cattle industry had to be shipped overland through the Andes to Panama—a 2,000-mile journey. Similarly, much-needed imports could not be brought by ship directly to Buenos Aires but had to pass through Panama, before being forwarded by the same long and dangerous route. As a result of this imposition, Buenos Aires became a smugglers' haven and headquarters for a profitable trade in illegal goods.

Many of Argentina's commercial harbors were constructed during the nineteenth century, emphasizing the nation's early focus on import and export capabilities.

Photo by Robert M. Levine

At liberty to live how they wanted, these nineteenth-century gauchos took refuge in a broken-down cart *(right)*. Gauchos roamed the pampas as a way of life, fighting for survival and independence. A gaucho takes time from his adventurous lifestyle to chat with a woman *(below)*.

The early settlers of Argentina were in large part descended from Spanish colonists in Paraguay, many of whom had freely intermarried with Paraguay's Guarani Indians. From these mestizos, with their mixed Spanish-and-Indian background, came the first gauchos—the hardy cattle herders of the pampas. Both the gauchos and the smuggler merchants of Buenos Aires began to feel less and less satisfied with Spanish rule.

The Spaniards finally recognized the need for local government in the colonies along the Río de la Plata, and in 1776 Spain created the Viceroyalty of La Plata, with Buenos Aires as its capital. Spain made the city a free port, permitting goods to enter and leave the country without taxing them. With this new freedom and authority, Buenos Aires began to prosper, and both its commerce and its population increased.

Independence

Although Buenos Aires thrived under the more relaxed Spanish rule, its people were still not content to remain governed by an overseas power. The successful revolt of Britain's colonies in North America and the spirit of equality that fueled the French Revolution encouraged many of the Argentine colonists to question the right of Spanish monarchs to control their affairs.

In the meantime, Napoleon Bonaparte had conquered half of Europe. In 1804 the French ruler entered into an alliance with Spain, and together the two countries declared war on Great Britain. In 1806, after the British defeated the combined French and Spanish fleets off Trafalgar, a British expeditionary force occupied Buenos Aires to establish a foothold in the region. The colonists, under Santiago de Liniers and Martín de Alzaga, rose up in arms and expelled the British. When France invaded Spain in 1808, the preoccupied Spanish government left Buenos Aires to run its own affairs.

By 1810 the colonists had acquired a taste for self-rule. They organized their own independent government under a council of local citizens to administer the Viceroyalty of La Plata. The provinces outside Argentina, however, opposed this action. Eventually they split into separate territories that went on to establish their own independence.

José de San Martín

In 1812 one of South America's great liberators, José de San Martín, came on the scene. Born in 1778 in the Argentine province of Misiones, San Martín had served the Spanish king in Europe during the Napoleonic Wars. Returning to his homeland in 1812, he offered his services to Argentina and organized and trained an army to secure independence. San Martín realized that the best way to gain independence was to drive Spain from all of its South American colonies, but especially from Peru, the stronghold of Spanish power in the Americas.

On July 9, 1816, representatives from the provinces that formed the Viceroyalty of La Plata attended the Congress of Tucumán, where they signed the Declaration of Independence, officially freeing Argentina from Spain.

This painting illustrates the Battle of Maipo on April 5, 1818, when San Martín and his forces destroyed the Spanish strongholds in southern South America.

After declaring Argentine independence at the Congress of Tucumán, San Martín led his troops across the Andes and stormed into Chile. With the aid of the Chilean patriot Bernardo O'Higgins, San Martín defeated the Spaniards in the Battle of Chacabuco in 1817 and subsequently triumphed over the remaining Spanish forces in Chile at Maipo. After resting his army, San Martín sailed with his men to the southern coast of Peru. Lima fell to San Martín in 1821, and he was declared "Protector of Peru." Simon Bolívar—who freed the remainder of Peru and the area that is now Ecuador, Colombia, Panama, Bolivia, and Venezuela—completed the conquest of the rest of Spain's South American possessions.

Civil Strife

While San Martín was leading his forces to victory, the territories of La Plata were torn by internal disagreement. The council leaders broke into factions and fought one another. Buenos Aires became the headquarters of the Unitarist party, which sought to centralize control in the capital city and to regulate the affairs of the outlying regions. In rural areas of the country the Federalist party was dominant. Composed mostly of ranchers, this party aimed to limit the control of the merchants of Buenos Aires and to establish a federal union of the various regions of the country. The conflicts between urban and rural regions halted Argentine trade and eco-

José de San Martín was instrumental in liberating Argentina, Chile, and Peru from Spanish colonialism.

nomic life, and the newly independent country seemed destined to split into separate territories.

In 1826 the Unitarist party drew up a constitution that affirmed the control of Buenos Aires over the interior and elected Bernardino Rivadavia president. Rivadavia encouraged foreign trade and distributed public land to improve agricultural output. But Rivadavia—a *porteño* (resident of the port city of Buenos Aires)—did not understand life in the interior, and his agricultural program failed. He was overthrown and the Federalists assumed control of the government. Their leader, Manuel Dorrego, was assassinated in a Unitarist coup.

Juan Manuel de Rosas ruled Argentina for 23 years. Although a tyrant, Rosas aroused a strong sense of nationalism among Argentines.

Juan Manuel de Rosas

Juan Manuel de Rosas, a Federalist sympathizer who was determined to end political feuding and to unite his fellow citizens, intervened. Ruling as a dictator from 1829 until 1852, he often employed ruthless methods to stop dissent. For example, he created a network of secret police to spy on his enemies and led violent campaigns against the Indians.

In spite of Rosas's Federalist beginnings, he succeeded in concentrating political power in Buenos Aires. Rosas interfered in the affairs of Uruguay and Bolivia and

This mid-nineteenth-century painting illustrates Argentine naval ships.

The battlefront of the War of the Triple Alliance—in which the forces of Argentina, Brazil, and Uruguay joined to fight against Paraguay—is depicted in this historical painting.

antagonized Great Britain and France, causing them to blockade Buenos Aires. Argentine trade suffered greatly as a result, and finally popular disapproval led to a rebellion headed by Justo José de Ur-

Bartolomé Mitre, a fugitive from Rosas's regime, worked as a journalist in several South American countries before reestablishing Buenos Aires as the capital and becoming president of Argentina.

quiza. With Brazilian aid, Urquiza forced Rosas into exile in 1852.

Making a Nation

Representatives from all Argentine provinces—except Buenos Aires—met at Santa Fe and wrote a new constitution, patterned after that of the United States. The constitution established a confederation of the provinces, named the city of Paraná as the federal government seat, and severely limited the central control of Buenos Aires. Urquiza was elected president of the new confederation.

Once again the domination of Buenos Aires became an important issue. Unwilling to accept the loss of their power and privileges, the rich merchants of Buenos Aires refused to join the new federation and maintained a semi-independent status for almost a decade. Civil war broke out when Urquiza tried to force Buenos Aires to join the federation, but in 1861 a Buenos Aires army led by General Bartolomé Mitre defeated Urquiza's forces. In 1862 Buenos Aires entered the federation on its own terms. Among these terms

This stone engraving of a parrot head, dating from about A.D. 100, is one of many pre-Columbian artifacts excavated from Argentina's coast.

was the restoration of its status as the nation's capital.

After a century of disorder and dictatorship, Argentina began to prosper. Mitre was elected president in 1862, beginning a period of stable government that lasted nearly 70 years. Both he and his successor, Domingo Faustino Sarmiento, attracted European investment and immigrants, who opened up much of the pampas to agriculture. Sarmiento worked hard to bring public education to all parts of the nation. The only foreign conflict of the late nineteenth century took place from 1865 to 1870, when Argentina joined Brazil and Uruguay to defeat Paraguay in the War of the Triple Alliance.

Waves of immigrants from Europe settled in Argentina. Foreign trade flourished and irrigation schemes brought productivity to the arid west. The development of the country's vast agricultural wealth increased, and, as in other South American countries, agriculture shaped the economy. The remaining Indian tribes were beaten and scattered, and railways were built to transport farm produce from the pampas to Buenos Aires.

But unlike other South American countries, in Argentina few Indians inhabited the land. Thus Argentina did not follow the Latin American pattern of developing a huge lower class of Indians and mestizos who were ruled by a small aristocracy of European descent.

Reform Movements

During the late nineteenth century, political reforms began in Argentina. An energetic group of Argentines, dissatisfied with the wealthy, conservative officials who controlled the government, set up an opposition group called the Unión Cívica. This organization later became the Radical party, which appealed to many immigrants and middle-class Argentines.

Roque Sáenz Peña, who was elected president in 1910, finally succeeded in pushing election reforms through congress. The new law—known as the Sáenz Peña Law—prevented large landholders from controlling elections and established the secret ballot for eligible voters—men over the age of 18. In the country's first democratic election under the Sáenz Peña Law, Hipólito Irigoyen—leader of the Radical party—was elected president in 1916. The Radical party maintained control from 1916 to 1930, replacing many members of the legislature who had been part of the traditional, wealthy ruling class. As part of this shift in control, the middle class began to have more influence on national issues.

After World War I Argentina's economy continued to flourish. With good times, social legislation was enacted, and public works projects were launched on an impressive scale. Irigoyen instituted labor reforms, including a minimum wage law and annual paid vacations for railroad workers. He also introduced university reforms that allowed for freedom of thought, that fired incompetent teachers, and that gave students a voice in university government.

In 1930 Irigoyen was overthrown by military leaders who resented his domination of Argentine politics. The country has often been ruled by military dictatorships since then. Irigoyen's overthrow came at the beginning of an economic slump and a period of social unrest. During this time Argentina, like much of the rest of the world, suffered through the Great Depression.

A trend toward conservative politics dominated Argentine life through the beginning of World War II. When hostilities broke out in Europe in 1939, Argentina declared itself neutral and maintained

Turn-of-the-century immigrants socialize in the dining room of a hotel in Buenos Aires.

Hipólito Irigoyen and the Radical party dominated Argentine politics from 1916 until 1930, when he was ousted from office by a coup d'état. The rebels became the first militant group in 70 years of national history to overthrow the Argentine government.

Photo by Robert M. Levine

diplomatic relations with the Axis powers—Germany, Italy, and Japan—even though most other nations of the Western Hemisphere had severed ties with the Axis countries. Opinions about World War II were sharply divided within Argentina. There were large numbers of Argentines of Italian and German background, some of whom sympathized with the Axis. Those who favored strict neutrality confronted those who wished the government to align itself with Britain, the United States, and the Allies. It was not until 1945—at the end of the war—that Argentina declared war on the Axis powers.

Juan Domingo Perón

In 1943 a military junta seized control of the Argentine government. A second mil-

itary coup followed in 1944, bringing into the political spotlight a man who would lead Argentina for several years—Juan Domingo Perón. Perón, an army colonel, served as a minister of labor in the junta government, a position he used to influence Argentine politics. By increasing the pay and benefits of wage earners, Perón won the support of urban workers—a group that had been ignored by previous governments.

In 1946 Perón was elected president of Argentina. Shortly thereafter his supporters formed the Peronist party, which has influenced Argentine politics ever since. As a friend of labor, Perón continued to give economic and political voice to the working class and helped to form the powerful General Confederation of Labor. Eventually he raised the proportion of

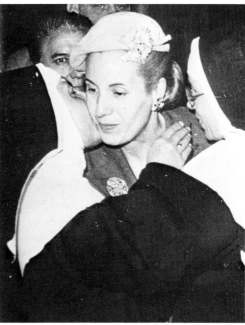

President Juan Domingo Perón *(left)* extended Argentine influence throughout Latin America. Eva Duarte de Perón *(right)*, his second wife, was often considered the mastermind of the president's political strategy. Grateful for the charitable contributions Eva gathered, the Roman Catholic Church supported the Peróns until Juan antagonized it by interfering with the Church's influence over the unions.

The masses, composed of the urban working class, idolized Eva because she initiated policies to benefit their welfare. Eva, in turn, could rely on their support to quell anti-Peronists. In 1945, shortly before Juan Perón was elected president, a disenchanted military kidnapped him. He was released soon after, when laborers, beseeched by Eva, threatened the capital with disorderly conduct and a general strike.

union workers within the total labor force from one-tenth to two-thirds.

Perón was greatly assisted by his second wife, Eva Duarte de Perón, who helped to organize the labor movement. Eva Perón commanded such popular appeal that workers in large cities held mass demonstrations of support and affection for "Evita," as they fondly called her. Eva Perón also mobilized women, gaining them the right to vote in 1947 and founding women's political and social-service organizations. The Eva Duarte de Perón Foundation provided financial assistance to widows, orphans, the sick, the handicapped, and the poor.

ECONOMIC DECLINE

President Perón sought to develop Argentine industry and to create a more balanced economy. But in seeking this end, he allowed the nation's agricultural sector to decline. Although he instituted a program to provide low-cost housing for urban workers, he did nothing to break up the holdings of large landowners and to redistribute farmland among the middle and lower classes—despite promises to create land-reform programs. A tax on farm products, which was used to strengthen industry, further stifled agricultural growth. As a result, farm production dropped and the nation's income fell.

Nevertheless, Perón continued to increase government spending. His first Five-Year Plan further drained the nation's budget. The plan's goals were to purchase private- and foreign-owned transportation and public works, to speed up

Courtesy of Inter-American Development Bank

During his efforts to strengthen Argentina's industrial sector, President Perón did little to improve the output of the fertile pampas.

The Buenos Aires water authority is housed in this ornate structure. As a result of Perón's Five-Year Plan, control of the water supply was taken from private ownership and placed in state hands.

the industrialization of Argentina, and to strengthen the nation's international power and prestige.

As disapproval of Perón's regime increased, he pulled the reins of power tighter and suspended freedoms of the press and speech. He changed the constitution to increase his control over Argentina and to allow him to run for a second term of office. But Perón's power declined during his second term, as his initial popularity waned. He already had alienated estate owners, businesspeople, middle-class supporters of the Radical party, and left-wing socialists. Eventually, he also lost the support of the Roman Catholic Church by limiting its authority.

In 1955 a military revolt overthrew Perón, and he fled to Spain. By that time the country was nearly bankrupt. Although Perón's economic and social plan to convert Argentina into a modern industrial state could have greatly benefited the na-

tion, his hunger for complete power undermined his plan.

Disrupted Political Climate

The governments that followed Perón faced increasing social unrest—riots, revolts, strikes, bombings—as the Argentine cost of living began to soar. With high expectations for a prosperous lifestyle, many Argentines continued to make labor and social welfare demands, despite the nation's dwindling economic growth. About one-fourth of the population—primarily trade union workers—remained loyal to Perón. These supporters of Perón—called Peronists—organized many disturbances.

In 1956 Perón's Constitution of 1949 was replaced with the original Constitution of 1853. Free press was also restored, but the Peronists were banned from political activity, which limited the ability of the government to enlist popular support.

Members of the Patrician Regiment, the most prestigous infantry of the Argentine army, wear a traditional uniform to commemorate the victory in 1806 of the Buenos Aires militia over the British army.

Monument to the Workers, located in Buenos Aires on Paseo Colón, honors the Argentine working class.

When Arturo Frondizi of the Radical party was elected president in 1958, he set about reviving the nation's economy. Frondizi sought to curb inflation and to lower the nation's debt by cutting governmental spending and by decreasing wage hikes. These measures, however, called for financial sacrifices and the people disliked them. When the Peronist party won 34 percent of the vote in the 1962 elections, the armed forces overthrew Frondizi, fearing he would submit to Peronist pressures to restore Perón's economic policies.

For the next decade the Argentine government shifted between civilian presidents and military dictators. By the late 1960s the country's worsening economy again resulted in strikes, violence, and antigovernment protests. In 1973 army leaders allowed a Peronist—Héctor José Cámpora—to return to power, hoping that he would be able to restore order. Later that year Perón returned from Spain; Cámpora resigned, paving the way for Perón's reelection in October. When the aging Perón died in office the following year, he was succeeded by his third wife, Isabel, who had held the vice presidency.

Politically inexperienced, Isabel Perón was unable to deal with Argentina's deteriorating economy, a situation that would have challenged even the most seasoned and skillful politician. The inflation rate soared to a new world record of over 400 percent. Terrorists threatened the nation's people daily. In 1976 military leaders arrested Isabel Perón and took over the government.

The "Dirty War"

The unstable economy, joblessness, and high inflation led to increasingly violent demonstrations against the military rule. In an effort to root out political dissent, the junta, headed by General Jorge Rafael Videla, mounted a vicious campaign—which became known as the "dirty war"—that violated many of the people's civil rights. During successive military regimes of the late 1970s and early 1980s, some authorities estimate that between 15,000 and 30,000 Argentines were kidnapped and tortured by military officials—never to be heard from again. Although some of these people—called *desaparecidos* (the disappeared)—doubtless participated in terrorist acts, many of them were innocent of any crime.

Speaking for the military in 1979, Gen-

In October 1973 Juan Perón again became president of Argentina. Pictured with him is his third wife, Isabel, who served as vice president during his administration.

Independent Picture Service

39

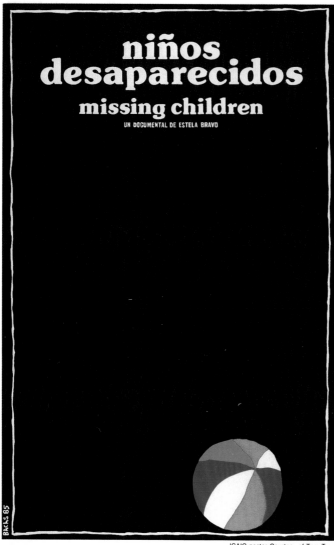

niños desaparecidos
missing children
UN DOCUMENTAL DE ESTELA BRAVO

The military's brutal treatment of those they believed opposed them inspired the Cuban film *niños desaparecidos* (missing children). The award-winning movie focused on the orphaned children of thousands of citizens who were unjustly jailed, tortured, and killed. The government put the orphans up for adoption without the knowledge or approval of their relatives.

ICAIC poster Courtesy of Tom Trow

eral Roberto Viola declared that "like all wars, this one has left tremendous wounds that only time can heal. There are the dead, the wounded, the jailed, and those who are absent forever. Don't ask for explanations where there are none." But Argentines were not to be silenced. More and more relatives of the desaparecidos gathered to inquire about the fate of their loved ones and to protest repression.

In 1980 Adolfo Pérez Esquivel was awarded the Nobel Prize for peace in recognition of his work to track down Argentines who had disappeared. The following year saw publication of *Prisoner Without a Name, Cell Without a Number* by Jacobo Timmerman. An Argentine newspaper editor, Timmerman had been treated brutally while under detention by the Argentine military authorities. In his book, which called the situation in Argentina to world attention, Timmerman charged that the country's military was not only brutal in repressing dissent, but also anti-Semitic, striking out against him partly because he was a Jew.

The Falkland Islands War

Led by Leopoldo Galtieri, the Argentine military further shocked world opinion on April 2, 1982, by sending armed forces to seize and occupy the Falkland Islands, a British colony about 300 miles off the coast of southern Argentina. Argentina had first claimed the Islas Malvinas—the Argentine name for the Falklands—in 1820. Having at that time recently gained independence from Spain, Argentina felt that it was the rightful successor to Spanish rule. In 1833, however, Great Britain assumed control of the islands. The dispute that resulted has never been resolved.

The Argentine military leaders thought the invasion would be a successful blow against colonialism, a motive that they hoped all of Latin America would support. But the military government was also using the invasion as a means to unite disillusioned Argentines behind a popular, nationalistic cause. The action was seen by some observers as a last desperate move by the military to focus the people's attention away from an economy that was on the brink of collapse.

The military, however, had not anticipated the quick and forceful response of the British. The invasion led to a ten-week

Courtesy of Minneapolis Public Library and Information Center

Sheep greatly outnumber people on the British-held Falkland Islands.

war in which Britain gathered a powerful fleet and defeated Argentine troops—who lost about 750 lives during the war—near Port Stanley, the islands' capital. Nevertheless, both Britain and Argentina refuse to give up their claims, and a settlement has yet to be negotiated.

Return to Democracy

Argentina emerged from the ill-advised Falklands War with a mushrooming foreign debt of more than $40 billion and an annual inflation rate of 137 percent. Argentines demanded change, and the provisional government kept its promise to return the country to civilian, democratic rule. Raúl Alfonsín, who assumed office in 1983, had campaigned as a supporter of democracy and a champion of human rights.

As president, Alfonsín immediately took steps to reorganize Argentina's armed forces. He attempted to rid the military of officers who had participated in the dirty war. He also punished those who continued to speak out against reductions in the nation's bloated defense budget. At the same time, Alfonsín sought to curb the power of the trade unions by cutting the increases in workers' wages. Once firmly in power, Alfonsín obtained pledges of national unity from Isabel Perón and the leaders from 15 other political parties.

To fulfill his promises in the field of human rights, Alfonsín's administration brought former military junta leaders to trial on charges of officially approved murder, torture, and kidnapping during their administrations. At the same time, the junta leaders during the Falklands War were brought to trial and accused of

The Argentine peso has increased in value since the Alfonsín administration was elected in 1985.

Courtesy of R.D. Research

42

Casa Rosada (Pink House) is the official residence of the president of Argentina.

mismanagement of the conflict. The courts handed many of the former junta leaders stiff jail sentences.

In the early years of his term, Alfonsín successfully grappled with the nation's severe economic problems. In 1985 he introduced the Austral Plan, which halted wage and price increases and put an end to the long-standing practice of printing extra money to cover government spending. But the nation's people were not ready to make the sacrifices necessary to restore the economy, and Alfonsín was not prepared to enforce his program. By 1987 inflation had begun to increase once again, and support for Alfonsín declined.

Elections in the spring of 1989 brought a Peronist, Carlos Raúl Menem to power. As a member of the Peronist party, Menem enjoyed wide popularity. But to tackle the nation's economic troubles, he will have to turn from traditional Peronist policies, which favor the working class at the expense of the national budget. It remains to be seen whether Menem will succeed in making economic reforms while maintaining the support of the Argentine people.

Governmental Structure

With the return to democracy in 1983, Argentina restored its Constitution of 1853. The Argentine government is organized as a federal republic whose highest powers reside in executive, legislative, and judicial branches. With the checks and balances created by this division of power, no individual should be able to assume complete control.

As provided by the constitution, the president and vice president are elected for a term of six years and may not serve a second consecutive term. Both officials must be Roman Catholic and Argentine by birth. The president is commander in chief of the armed services and appoints all civil

43

and judicial officeholders. The president is assisted by the vice president and a cabinet of eight ministers, who are also appointed by the president.

A bicameral (two-house) legislature consists of a senate and a chamber of deputies. The senate is composed of 46 members—two representing each province and two from the federal district of Buenos Aires. The provincial legislatures elect federal senators, with the exception of the senators from Buenos Aires, who are elected by the people. Senators serve nine-year terms, and one-third come up for reelection every three years. The chamber of deputies has 254 members, who are elected by the people. All Argentines 18 years of age or older are eligible to vote. Deputies serve four-year terms, and half come up for reelection every two years.

In accord with constitutional procedure, the legislature can legally remove the president, vice president, and cabinet members from office. The president may refuse to sign laws passed by the legislature, but his veto may be overridden by a two-thirds vote in each house.

At the top of Argentina's judiciary is its supreme court, which is made up of five judges who are appointed by the president with the approval of the senate. The supreme court has the power to declare legislative acts unconstitutional. The president also appoints judges of the federal courts of appeal. Each province has its own supreme court and lower courts.

Argentina is divided into 22 provinces, 1 island territory (Tierra del Fuego), and 1 federal district, all of which exercise local government. Each province elects its own governor and legislature, while the president appoints the governor of Tierra del Fuego. An elected mayor heads the federal district of Buenos Aires.

Artwork by Jim Simondet

The Argentine flag, with its three horizontal stripes, became official when the country gained independence in 1816. The "Sun of May," in the center, was added in 1818 to depict the sun shining through the clouds of Buenos Aires on May 25, 1810, when Argentines first demonstrated against the Spanish viceroy.

Approximately 85 percent of Argentines are descendants of Spanish or Italian immigrants. ✗

3) The People

Of Argentina's 31.9 million people, 97 percent are of European ancestry. Most of these people have Spanish or Italian backgrounds, but many immigrants also have come from Great Britain or from other European countries. Since the 1970s most of Argentina's immigrants have arrived from neighboring countries—especially Bolivia, Chile, and Paraguay—for political or economic reasons.

Before the great waves of European settlers came over in the second half of the nineteenth century, most of Argentina's population lived in the east central region near Buenos Aires. This part of the country is still the most densely populated, containing not only several of the largest cities but also numerous small villages.

Irrigation, however, has now opened up much of the interior to farming, and many new immigrants have settled in this region. Sheep raising and, later, petroleum exploitation, brought some people into the chilly south, but the population is still sparse in Patagonia and Tierra del Fuego.

Many groups typical of old Argentina have all but disappeared. Very few blacks remain, though in colonial days large

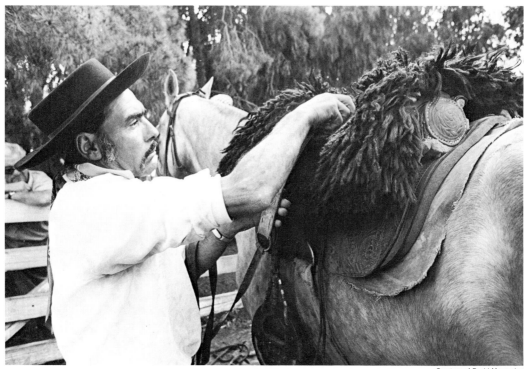

Although the true, rough-and-rugged gauchos of Argentina remain only in legend, a few cowboys still carry on the gaucho tradition.

numbers of Africans were brought in as slaves. Groups of Indians and gauchos, rough-riding cowboys, are much smaller than they once were. Only about 50,000 pure Indians still live in Argentina. Of these, most inhabit the isolated areas of the Andes, the Gran Chaco, Patagonia, and Tierra del Fuego.

The Gauchos

Like cowboys of the North American Wild West, Argentina's old-time gauchos, who were often mestizos, fought against Indians and the forces of nature. As settlers of a hostile environment, gauchos were suspicious of life in the cities. They were self-reliant, extremely tough, and distrustful of authority, but they were always ready to follow a strong leader.

These cowboys led uncomplicated lives and took care of basic needs in simple ways.

They often made boots from the hide of a freshly killed colt, removing the skin from the animal's hind legs and slipping it over their own legs and feet to dry and assume the shape of a boot. In addition to colt-skin boots, gauchos wore bombachas (balloon trousers) and broad-brimmed hats.

Gauchos ate meat almost exclusively, living on fresh beef and charqui (jerky)—meat that is preserved by drying it in the sun. They drank yerba mate (holly tea) throughout the day. Stored in a hollowed-out gourd, mate was sipped through a metal straw called a bombilla.

Hostile to Spanish rule and conscious of Argentine nationalism, gauchos represented the Argentine spirit of the colonial period. Scorning crowds of people and European influences, these roughriders resented the new immigrants of the nineteenth century who swarmed onto the pampas and fenced in the open range. The modernization of Argentina's interior has made the traditional life of the gaucho virtually a thing of the past.

Although some Argentines who live in the country continue gaucho traditions, they are just a few among thousands of employees engaged in the modern, scientific breeding and raising of Argentine beef. Nevertheless, the image of the gaucho survives as a symbol of Argentine strength and individualism.

The Criollos

Much of the character of Argentine life, especially in the interior provinces, is taken from the criollos (Creoles). In colonial days this term meant people born in Argentina of Spanish parentage. Later, criollo was used to distinguish the Argentines of colonial descent from the offspring of nineteenth-century European immigrants. These newcomers were readily absorbed, however, and criollo now usually means an Argentine who lives in the country or in a small town.

The early criollos, accustomed to neglect by Spain and to mismanagement by Spanish colonial administrators, developed a strong sense of self-reliance and, in time, a sense of being Argentine rather than Spanish. This frontier spirit, like the gaucho spirit, is very much present in the Argentine national outlook. Argentines

Farmers—often called criollos—produce the bulk of Argentina's wealth.

tend to be proud, hospitable, and courteous, but they also possess an element of strong independence. European immigrants, dissatisfied with conditions in their home countries, found in Argentina a new, South American identity on which to build a new life.

Food

Although rural diets vary less than urban ones, the natural bounty of Argentina's land assures that its people are well nourished. Beef is the basis of the Argentine diet—some people eat it three times a day. Perhaps the most popular dish in Argentina is asado, a beef roast or barbecue. Open-air barbecues often feature asado con cuero, an entire steer roasted in its hide over an open fire, or, on a more modest scale, asado al asador, an entire lamb cooked in the same way.

Other popular beef dishes include *bife a caballo* (steak topped with a fried egg) and churrasco (grilled steak). *Punchero,* a stew of chicken, chick-peas, marrow bones, and vegetables, is a hearty dish. Italian immigrants introduced pasta dishes such as spaghetti to the Argentine diet. Tea time —a custom introduced by the British— offers many Argentines an afternoon break for tea and a snack.

Photo by Robert W. Nelson

Whole lambs are roasted at this Buenos Aires restaurant.

The nineteenth-century Argentine artist Prilidiano Pueyrredón depicts the life of the nation's early immigrants in *Un Alto en el Camino* (A Stop on the Way).

An Argentine meal might begin with empanadas (little pastries that are filled with meat, fish, or other seafood), which are also served as snacks. The most common desserts consist of fresh fruit and cheese. Prepared desserts include pastries, rice pudding, and *dulce de leche*—a mixture of sugar and milk. Coffee, yerba maté, beer, and domestic wines from the provinces of Río Negro and Mendoza are the customary beverages.

Language and Literature

Spanish is the official language of Argentina. Argentine Spanish, however, differs significantly from Castilian Spanish, the official language of Spain. Many Argentines also speak a second European language and read one of the foreign language newspapers printed daily in Buenos Aires. Of the surviving Indians, only a few still speak their native tongue.

Buenos Aires is one of the world's main distribution points for information printed in Spanish and for many years surpassed Madrid and Barcelona in the volume of books published. Printing and publishing are still significant activities in Argentina.

During the nineteenth century, gaucho themes and legends inspired many Argentine writers. A classic work read widely in Argentina and neighboring South American countries is *Martín Fierro*. In this epic poem José Hernández glorifies the heroic struggle of gauchos who rebel against society to preserve both the land and their individual freedom. Later writers who followed in Hernández's footsteps include Benito Lynch and Ricardo Güiraldes.

Jorge Luis Borges created a more universal style than his predecessors by combining an Argentine identity with European traditions. Borges gained international praise in the mid-twentieth century for his essays, poems, and short stories. Considered by many critics to be the most outstanding contemporary literary figure in the Spanish-speaking world, Borges is noted for his brilliant use of language and for original observations about the meaning of life. *Ficciónes* is perhaps his most important collection of short stories.

The Arts

Although echoes of Spain are everywhere, there is a pronounced French influence in

49

On Florida Street, which is reserved for pedestrians, Argentines meet in the late afternoon to talk, eat, drink, and shop.

These homes in La Boca, the colorful, old port district of Buenos Aires, house many Argentine artists.

Argentine cultural life. Buenos Aires actually resembles Paris more than Madrid in the style of architecture, the tempo of city life, and the pursuit of cultural activities. Argentine painting and music owe as much to Paris, Vienna, and Berlin as to Spain. In the nineteenth century, Argentine intellectuals flocked to universities in northern and central Europe and returned to their native land to apply the concepts and techniques they had learned abroad.

Thus Argentine artistic themes tend to be international rather than national, and much of the artistic output reflects art for its own sake rather than for social commentary. The first important painter in Argentina, Prilidiano Pueyrredón, depicted gaucho scenes during the nineteenth cen-

tury. Contemporary art has become much more experimental—often influenced by the United States—and breaks the distinction between painting and sculpture.

Argentine musicians have also looked to other countries for guidance. Alberto Williams, an early twentieth-century composer and founder of the Buenos Aires conservatory of music, was a student of the French composer César Franck. An outstanding contemporary composer is Alberto Ginastera, who draws from gaucho songs and dances. Audiences have been stunned by the violent, spectacular quality of Ginastera's opera *Bomarzo*.

A lively cultural capital, Buenos Aires hosts a year-round calendar of opera, ballet, concerts, and theatrical productions,

The Colón Theater, constructed from 1887 to 1908, is considered the finest concert hall in Latin America. Enthusiastic theatergoers, Argentines always fill the house for ballet and opera performances.

Courtesy of Museum of Modern Art of Latin America

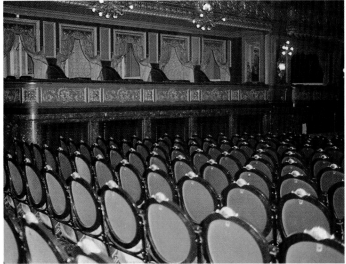

Gold-trimmed seats of red plush fabric adorn the interior of Buenos Aires's Colón Theater and face a stage that is as long as a city block.

Courtesy of Museum of Modern Art of Latin America

Outdoor theaters are common in Buenos Aires. The colorful buildings in the background are houses. From the convenience of their homes, nearby La Boca residents are able to watch performances.

which are supported by a strong public interest in the arts. Buenos Aires is the home of several symphony orchestras, including the Philharmonic Orchestra of Buenos Aires, the National Symphonic Orchestra, and the permanent orchestra of the Colón Theater.

Argentina is known as the home of the tango, a spirited dance that gained worldwide popularity in the years before World War I. Some authorities say the tango originated among Spanish gypsies and was brought to Argentina by the Spanish settlers, where it took on an Argentine flavor. Others hold that it is derived from the milonga, an Argentine ballroom dance that was popular in the early twentieth century.

Religion and Education

Over 90 percent of the Argentine population is Roman Catholic, though many do not actively practice their religion. Although freedom of religion is guaranteed by the constitution, the Catholic Church receives financial support from the government. Protestants make up about 2 percent of the population. Another 2 percent is Jewish, centered mainly in Buenos Aires. By far the largest Jewish community in Latin America, it is also the second largest in the New World.

Education is free and compulsory for children between the ages of 6 and 14. The literacy rate of 94 percent is, along with Uruguay's rate, the highest in Latin America. Compulsory public education is the responsibility of each provincial government. Federal funds, however, help to support the provincial school systems. The country also has many private schools, which charge tuition.

Secondary education is not required by law, and only a small percentage of children complete high school. Most high schools are operated by the federal government, although some are attached to Argentine universities. All universities are public and receive federal support. With about 40 universities, Argentina attracts students from several Latin American countries. The University of Córdoba, founded in 1613, is one of the oldest in the New World. With an enrollment of over 100,000 students, the University of Buenos Aires is the largest on the South American continent.

Courtesy of David Mangurian

The couple in this poster demonstrate the tango, a ballroom dance characterized by long steps and dramatic poses.

Sports

Argentines are very sports-minded. Soccer is the nation's most popular sport, and horse racing is a close second. Argentine racetracks are among the world's best, and a large segment of the public lives, breathes, and talks horses. Sports involving horsemanship, such as polo and the rough-and-tumble sport called *pato,* are extremely popular. In pato, horseback riders attempt to toss a six-handled ball into a high basket.

Clubs and sporting associations thrive everywhere, and golf, tennis, swimming, and other water sports have large followings. Argentina has produced champions in all of these activities. Rural areas offer limitless opportunities for skiing, hiking, camping, hunting, and fishing. The long coastline and many lakes are ideal for yachting and boating. The climate of much of the country encourages outdoor activities.

Trout can grow to be quite large in the waters of Chubut province, as this proud fisherman will attest. Argentines enjoy plentiful fishing, in part because their fisheries have not been fully exploited by the industry.

A *pato* player swoops down and retrieves the game's sought-after, inflated leather bag. A sport that originated in Argentina and that initially was played using the body of a duck *(pato),* pato combines elements of polo and basketball. Two teams mounted on horseback struggle to catch the leather bag, carry it down the field, and hurl it into the goal zone.

Machines do most of the heavy work on farms of the pampas.

Courtesy of Inter-American Development Bank

4) The Economy

With the rich and fertile land of the pampas—the nation's most important natural resource—Argentina once had a very stable economy and a comfortable standard of living. Since Perón's rise to power in 1947, however, Argentina's economy has spiraled steadily downward. Argentines still raise grains and beef that help feed the world, but strong industries have yet to be developed. Without competitive products to sell, the nation is a weak trader on the world market.

The working class has caused some of the economic troubles by not producing enough factory-made items to keep up with their demands for consumer goods and for increased wages. As a result, the government began to print extra money to pay the workers. This practice has caused inflation to soar. In the 1980s, the rate of inflation frequently exceeded 1,000 percent per year, crippling the nation's economy. Once known for its high standard of living and affordable food prices, Argentina now is watching many of its middle-class citizens slip into poverty.

President Carlos Menem, a Peronist, vowed to tackle Argentina's finances when he took office in 1989. Casting aside the Peronist tradition of steak on every table,

Argentina ranks among the top ten countries in the world for wheat production *(right)* and is fifth for cattle raising *(below)*.

Courtesy of Inter-American Development Bank

Courtesy of David Mangurian

55

Judges observe prize bulls at the National Livestock Show in Buenos Aires.

An inspector examines carcasses at a meat-processing plant. From here, beef products are sent to markets across the globe.

Menem prescribed a long, painful path of economic changes. By raising taxes, halting wage increases, and cutting government spending, Menem hopes to bring Argentina's economic problems under control.

Agriculture

Covering one-fifth of the country, the pampas rank—along with Iowa in the United States and the Ukraine in the Soviet Union—as one of the world's greatest expanses of fertile topsoil. Deep layers of sediment that filtered down from the Andes formed the pampas—a process that continues as fine, windblown material settles over the region and enriches the soil for each new crop. The soil of the pampas is highly organic. Some agricultural specialists speculate that the fertility of the pampas was increased by the pre-Colum-

bian practice of burning vegetation to prepare the ground for crop planting.

In a good year the Argentine pampas produce over 40 million tons of grain—principally wheat, corn, sorghum (a grain similar to Indian corn), soybeans, and sunflower seeds. In addition, the grasses of the pampas nourish more than 50 million cattle, which provide meat for export as well as for domestic consumption.

In recent years, life on the pampas has changed as large-scale agribusinesses have replaced the independent landowners and tenant farmers who worked the land during the first half of the twentieth century. Because political leaders since World War II have emphasized industrialization rather than agriculture, Argentine farmers have not been encouraged to keep up with the latest agricultural developments. As a result, Argentines now must upgrade the agricultural sector if they are to remain

Río Negro province, in central Argentina, produces some of the world's finest apples.

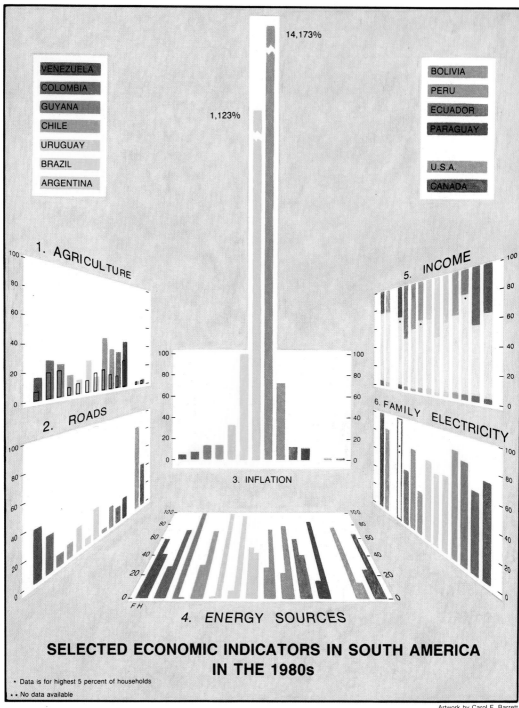

14,173%

1,123%

VENEZUELA
COLOMBIA
GUYANA
CHILE
URUGUAY
BRAZIL
ARGENTINA

BOLIVIA
PERU
ECUADOR
PARAGUAY

U.S.A.
CANADA

1. AGRICULTURE

2. ROADS

3. INFLATION

4. ENERGY SOURCES

5. INCOME

6. FAMILY ELECTRICITY

SELECTED ECONOMIC INDICATORS IN SOUTH AMERICA IN THE 1980s

* Data is for highest 5 percent of households

** No data available

Artwork by Carol F. Barrett

This multigraph depicts six important South American economic factors. The same factors for the United States and Canada are included for comparison. Data is from *1986 Britannica Book of the Year, Encyclopedia of the Third World, Europa Yearbook,* and *Countries of the World and their Leaders, 1987.*

In GRAPH 1—labeled Agriculture—the colored bars show the percentage of a country's total labor force that works in agriculture. The overlaid black boxes show the percentage of a country's gross domestic product that comes from agriculture. In most cases—except Argentina —the number of agricultural workers far exceeds the amount of income produced by the farming industry.

GRAPH 2 depicts the percentage of paved roads, while GRAPH 3 illustrates the inflation rate. The inflation figures for Colombia, Guyana, and Brazil are estimated. GRAPH 4 depicts two aspects of energy usage. The left half of a country's bar is the percentage of energy from fossil fuel (oil or coal); the right half shows the percentage of energy from hydropower. In GRAPH 5, which depicts distribution of wealth, each country's bar represents 100 percent of its total income. The top section is the portion of income received by the richest 10 percent of the population. The bottom section is the portion received by the poorest 20 percent. GRAPH 6 represents the percentage of homes that have electricity.

This man uses a monitor to determine the level of pollution in the air.

A farm couple of European descent bag potatoes for planting.

Manufacturing accounts for nearly 40 percent of Argentina's gross domestic product and employs one in five Argentine workers, including this man who works in a Buenos Aires tire factory.

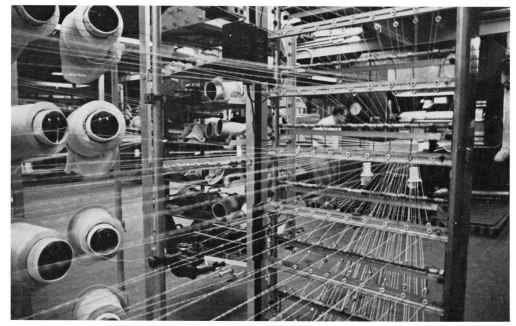

A machine twists rayon threads to form yarn. The yarn is then wound onto large bobbins that will be shipped to weaving mills.

competitive with other nations that have invested more heavily in the modernization of farming. In the 1980s, falling grain prices, as well as foreign competition, have hurt Argentina's profits from agriculture.

LIVESTOCK RAISING

Scientific breeding of animals was introduced in the mid-nineteenth century to satisfy the desires of Argentina's main customer—Britain—for fatter beef. At that time, stock of the finest pedigree was imported from Britain to improve Argentina's domestic herds, with the result that today the country is especially well known for the quality of its Black Angus and Hereford breeds.

Nearly 40 percent of Argentina's beef production is concentrated within the province of Buenos Aires, where cattle can be raised, slaughtered, and conveyed to market with minimal transportation costs. Other provinces that are leading livestock producers include La Pampa, Córdoba, Entre Ríos, and Santa Fe.

FARMING

Never as large an industry as cattle raising, farming was introduced largely by German, Dutch, and Swiss immigrants in the late nineteenth century. By that time the cattle industry had become large enough that grain production for cattle

A little boy in Jujuy province grasps a stalk of sugarcane. The stalk contains a sweet juice that will be refined into granulated sugar.

feed was important. The new European immigrants produced maize, wheat, flax, and alfalfa in quantities large enough to export as well as to feed livestock.

Today, in addition to these staples, crops of growing economic importance include sunflower seeds and soybeans, both of which are pressed for their oil. Fruit has also become a major crop. In the cooler, drier provinces in the western and southern extremes of the pampas, orchards of apples, pears, and plums thrive. There are also successful grape vineyards for wine making. Mesopotamia, the moist, rich heartland north of the pampas, specializes in citrus fruits, peaches, plums, and quinces (hard-fleshed, yellow apples used for jelly). Cotton, sugarcane, and yerba maté are the chief crops of the subtropical northern provinces; in Patagonia sheep are raised for their wool.

Industry

The processing of food and meat products is Argentina's most important industry. Industrialized since Perón rose to power in 1947, Argentina produces much of the nation's food requirements and fills most of its domestic needs for clothing, household equipment, and some types of machinery. Manufacturing accounts for 36 percent of Argentina's gross domestic product and employs about one-fifth of the country's workers.

Besides meat-packing and food-processing plants, manufacturing includes textile mills, companies that make leather prod-

Workers construct an irrigation project in the dry province of San Juan. The project is part of a resettlement program for farmers.

ucts, and, in the industrial city of Córdoba, factories that produce automobiles and railroad cars. Because of Argentina's large pool of skilled labor, foreign investors from Europe and the United States have formed partnerships with some Argentine industrialists to manufacture products for world markets. But the output of Argentine factory workers is low compared to other countries, which makes it hard for Argentine products to compete with foreign goods in international trade.

Energy Resources

In recent years Argentina has invested heavily in the development of its energy resources, including petroleum and hydroelectric power. About 70 percent of the energy used in Argentina comes from petroleum, with natural gas, coal, hydroelectricity, and nuclear power supplying the rest of the nation's energy. Hydroelectric power plants supply over 40 percent of the country's electricity.

Argentina leads all Latin American nations in the field of nuclear power. The country has two nuclear power plants in operation and three more under construction. Argentine progress in this field has been so rapid that the country is now providing assistance to other countries in developing their nuclear technology.

Strengthening the Private Sector

Until democracy was restored in 1983, the Argentine government assumed a domi-

Technical School Number One, pictured here under construction, was the first school built in a network of technical institutes being erected across the country.

nant position within the nation's economy. In the early 1970s it was estimated that government-operated companies were producing nearly one-half of the country's total output of goods and services. The estimate included companies that were completely government owned (airlines, petroleum complexes, and natural gas fields), as well as mixed-ownership companies in which the government was the dominant partner, such as the electrical utility that provided services to the metropolitan area of Buenos Aires.

Over the years, overstaffing and mismanagement of state-run companies have forced these businesses into serious debt. With the return to democracy in 1983, the Argentine government began selling to private investors companies that had been losing money under government control. In part this process was made necessary by the country's ballooning foreign debts, which by 1986 amounted to more than $50 billion.

The Future

Argentina's future depends on the ability of its government to bring the economy under control. Economic success, however, also hinges on the willingness of the Argentine people to undergo hardship for several years. Argentines must accept fixed wages and increased taxes to enable the government to rebuild the economy. The role of the military, which was greatly reduced during the term of President Alfonsín, may increase as President Menem strives to maintain order amid change. If Menem can succeed in lowering inflation and government spending over the long term, then Argentines may regain the high standard of living they once enjoyed.

Courtesy of Inter-American Development Bank

With the help of a tugboat, this barge lays a pipeline across the Strait of Magellan – the rough, narrow waterway that separates the islands of Tierra del Fuego from the rest of the South American continent. The pipeline will carry natural gas from the islands to the mainland.

Index